Books by Keith

The Intellect
Aphoris
Speculative Aphorisms
Speculative Aphorisms II
Philoscience
Philoscience II
Intellectual Jazz
Intellectual Jazz II
Jazzism
Neoliberal Arts
Neoliberal Arts II
Postmodern Minimalist Philosophy
Simpletism
Uncertaintyism
The Ultimate Truth
Anything Is Possible
Political and Social Observations
The University of Neoliberal Arts
A New Breed of Philosophers
Ferreirism - The Ultimate Philosophy
The eChurch of Zerotropy
The Ferreira Genesis Equation
Zerotropism and Panaceanism
Philosophy Should Belong to the Masses
Programming the World with Philosophy
The Masses Should Think for Themselves

Please visit my website at: *http://www.philophysics.com*
Thank You!

The Masses Educated Can Never Be Defeated

Keith N. Ferreira

iUniverse, Inc.
New York   Bloomington

The Masses Educated Can Never Be Defeated

iUniverse books may be ordered through booksellers or by contacting:

iUniverse
1663 Liberty Drive
Bloomington, IN 47403
www.iuniverse.com
1-800-Authors (1-800-288-4677)

Because of the dynamic nature of the Internet, any Web addresses or
links contained in this book may have changed since publication and
may no longer be valid. The views expressed in this work are solely
those of the author and do not necessarily reflect the views of the
publisher, and the publisher hereby disclaims any responsibility for
them.

ISBN: 978-1-4502-3846-5 (sc)
ISBN: 978-1-4502-3847-2 (ebook)

Printed in the United States of America

iUniverse rev. date: 07/26/2010

Table of Contents

The Masses Educated Can Never Be Defeated (Part One)

The Masses Educated Can Never Be Defeated (Part Two)

The Masses Educated Can Never Be Defeated (Part Three)

The Masses Educated Can Never Be Defeated (Part Four)

The Masses Educated Can Never Be Defeated (Part Five)

The Masses Educated Can Never Be Defeated (Part One)

The Masses Educated Can Never Be Defeated

The masses educated can never be defeated. Believe it or not! May the Source be with you! QED! (9/11/09)

Unpunctuated Consistency vs Punctuated Consistency

The only difference between science and religion is that the former believes that nature consists of unpunctuated consistency, while the latter believes that nature consists of punctuated consistency. Neither one is provable with absolute certainty, however, because we could all be in the mind of a desktop nonclassical computer, which would make both science and religion uncertain to say the least. Believe it or not! May the Source be with you! QED! (9/11/09)

The Ferreira Ulti-Fundamental Equation Is: Pi = 0/0 = X

The Ferreira Ulti-Fundamental Equation is: Pi = 0/0 = X, where X equals anything, and everything possible, including God, when the diameter of Pi equals zero, and the circumference of Pi equals zero, also. Believe it or not! May the Source be with you! QED! (9/12/09)

Launchism Is My New Philosophy, and I like It!

Launchism is my new philosophy, and I like it! The philosophy of launchism states that postmodern minimalist philosophy, aka Neoliberal Arts, is a means of launching individuals, countries, etc., on permanent upward mataphorical trajectories into the universe of ideas, and beyond. Believe it or not! May the Source be with you! QED! (9/13/09)

The Omni-Intellectual Jackpot = (Pi = 0/0 = X)

The Omni-intellectual Jackpot = (Pi = 0/0 = X), where X equals anything, and everything possible, including God, when the diameter of Pi equals zero, and the circumference of Pi equals zero, also. Believe it or not! May the Source be with you! QED! (9/13/09)

Breaking the Spell of Academia Over the Masses

My websites are about breaking the spell of academia over the masses, because academia is all about shit: GUTs = Grand Unified Theories. Believe it or not! May the Source be with you! QED! (9/14/09)

The Key to Solving the Mind Problem = The Concept of Concrete Abstractions

The key to solving the mind problem was the hypothesization of the concept of concrete abstractions, which is a novel concept that I discovered (invented). Concrete abstractions can be distinguished from abstract abstractions, which were once thought to be the only type of abstractions. Concrete abstractions are the percepts of the senses, while abstract abstractions are the percepts of the faculty of thought. Believe it or not! May the Source be with you! QED! (9/14/09)

The Christian Clergy and Philosophy

If the Christian clergy really thinks that Christ's message is not philosophical, then why is the Christian clergy so deep into philosophy? And, why would the Christian clergy deny the masses philosophy? Is it because the Christian clergy thinks that philosophy is too good for the masses? I think so. What do you think? After all, philosophy is the love of wisdom, and why shouldn't the masses love wisdom as much as the Christian clergy? Believe it or not! May the Source be with you! QED! (9/15/09)

The Heatsink Index of Space Might Be Decreasing

The heatsink index of space might be decreasing, which would mean that it was much greater in the past than it is now. Also, the heatsink index of space can be used to prove that the universe is not expanding, or contracting. Believe it or not! May the Source be with you! QED! (9/15/09)

The Hypocrisy of Christianity

Do Christians really believe that God judges people by the size of their accumulated wealth, etc.? If not, then why are the Christian clergy, etc., so interested in judging people by their accumulated wealth, etc.? I believe that it is because of the hypocrisy of Christianity. Believe it or not! May the Source be with you! QED! (9/15/09)

What Are the Entropy Values of Religious Texts?

What each religious person has to ask himself/herself is: What is (are) the entropy value(s) of the religious text(s) that he/she believes in?, because all religious texts have entropy values, according to the neolaw of entropy. It should be noted that, except for God, all existent entities, including religious texts, have nonzero entropy values, according to the neolaw of entropy. Believe it or not! May the Source be with you! QED! (9/16/09)

A Political Slogan Designed to Control the Masses

The political slogan: "The people united will never be defeated" was designed by intellectuals to control the masses without educating the masses, or giving the masses real power over their lives. But my political slogan: The masses educated can never be defeated -- is designed to educate the masses in Neoliberal Arts, aka postmodern minimalist philosophy, and by so doing, I hope to give the masses true power over their lives. Believe it or not! May the Source be with you! QED! (9/16/09)

Intellectuals Are not Really Interested in Educating the Masses

Intellectuals are not really interested in educating the masses. But, instead, intellectuals are interested in controlling and exploiting the masses, while keeping the masses ignorant and subservient to them. Believe it or not! May the Source be with you! QED! (9/16/09)

What Is the Practical Alternative to Neoliberal Arts?

What is the practical alternative to Neoliberal Arts, aka postmodern minimalist philosophy, for the education of the masses? And, why is it not being implemented, if there is such an alternative to Neoliberal Arts for the education of the masses? I believe that there is no practical alternative to Neoliberal Arts for the education of the masses. Believe it or not! May the Source be with you! QED! (9/16/09)

So-Called Miracles, etc., Can Never Be Ruled Out Completely

So-called miracles, etc., can never be ruled out completely, because our reality might not be fundamental in any sense whatsoever, due to the fact that we could all be in the mind of a desktop nonclassical computer, which would make our reality subject to possible punctuated consistency. Believe it or not! May the Source be with you! QED! (9/17/09)

Women and Blacks Cannot Do Philosophy

After searching my whole life, without success, for women and blacks who can do philosophy, I have come to the conclusion that women and blacks cannot do philosophy, because they lack the philosophy gene(s). If women and blacks have the philosophy gene(s), then the philosophy gene(s) is (are) not expressed in the active genetic makeup of women and blacks. Believe it or not! May the Source be with you! QED! (9/18/09)

The Claims by Blacks That They Invented Philosophy Are False

Because of the inability of modern blacks to do philosophy, I have come to the conclusion that the claims by blacks that they invented philosophy are false. Believe it or not! May the Source be with you! QED! (9/18/09)

Blacks Belong to the Past

Blacks belong to the past, and they know it. Believe it or not! May the Source be with you! QED! (9/19/09)

Global Beats on AOL Radio Is Still the Radio Station to Beat

http://player.play.it/player/aolPlayer.html?v=new3.11.87&
ur=1&us=1&id=748

Intellectual Activity of the Future

Intellectual activity of the future will consists of posing questions to PPCs, and then perceiving the answers given by the PPCs. Believe it or not! May the Source be with you! QED! (9/19/09)

The Virtual and Exchange Particles Catastrophe

Quantum mechanics leads inevitably to the virtual and exchange particles catastrophe, which states that each cubic inch of space contains an infinite number of virtual and exchange particles each instant of time, which is ridiculous to say the least. Believe it or not! May the Source be with you! QED! (9/19/09)

The Hypocrisy of Science

The hypocrisy of science can be illustrated quite vividly by the virtual and exchange particles catastrophe in quantum mechanics, because, according to quantum mechanics, every cubic inch of space contains an infinite number of virtual and exchange particles each instant of time, which is ridiculous to say the least. Believe it or not! May the Source be with you! QED! (9/19/09)

Perhaps, Neutrinos Can Be Slowed Down to Zero Velocity, Also

http://www.harvardscience.harvard.edu/engineering-technology/articles/light-and-matter-united-0 (9/20/09)

The Masses, Inc.

The masses should incorporate, because the only way to fight money is with money. However, the masses should not allow the elites of society to run their corporations for them, because, otherwise, the masses will find themselves back where they started. Believe it or not! May the Source be with you! QED! (9/20/09)

Theoretical Scientists, in General, Are Con Artists

Theoretical scientists, in general, are con artists, because they tweak their scientific theories to fit the experimental data, then they proclaim that their scientific theories have phenomenal degrees of accuracy. Believe it or not! May the Source be with you! QED! (9/20/09)

The Only Way to Fight Money Is with Money

The masses should incorporate, because the only way to fight money is with money. However, the masses should not allow the elites of society to run their corporations for them, because, otherwise, the masses will find themselves back where they started. Believe it or not! May the Source be with you! QED! (9/20/09)

Philosophy Is the Most Superior Form of Intellectual Activity Possible

Philosophy is the most superior form of intellectual activity possible, because it incorporates all kinds of intellectual activity, and it takes all kinds of intellectual activity to higher and higher levels of achievement. At least, that is what postmodern minimalist philosophy, aka Neoliberal Arts, tries to do, quite successfully, I might add. Believe it or not! May the Source be with you! QED! (9/20/09)

People Who Do not Like Philosophy Are Intellectual Chimpanzees

People who do not like philosophy are intellectual chimpanzees, because it is philosophy that gives humanity their humanity, due to the fact that philosophy is the most superior form of intellectual activity possible. Believe it or not! May the Source be with you! QED! (9/21/09)

The Only Thing That Separates Human Beings from Chimpanzees

If one is not educated in Neoliberal Arts, aka postmodern minimalist philosophy, then one is merely an intellectual chimpanzee, because the only thing that separates human beings from chimpanzees is an education in Neoliberal Arts, aka postmodern minimalist philosophy. Believe it or not! May the Source be with you! QED! (9/21/09)

The New Standard of What It Means to Be Human

The new standard of what it means to be human is to be educated in Neoliberal Arts, aka postmodern minimalist philosophy, as opposed to being a chimpanzee for not being educated in Neoliberal Arts, aka postmodern minimalist philosophy. Believe it or not! May the Source be with you! QED! (9/21/09)

It Is Highly Likely That Both Science and Religion Are Wrong

It is highly likely that both science and religion are wrong, and that postmodern minimalist philosophy, aka Neoliberal Arts, is right, because we could all really be in the mind of a desktop nonclassical computer. In other words, philosophy is superior to science and religion, because philosophy is pointing out how both science and religion could be wrong. Believe it or not! May the Source be with you! QED! (9/22/09)

Nothing Makes the Elites of Society More Nervous

Nothing makes the elites of society more nervous, than when the masses begin to show some interest in philosophy. I would like the masses to ponder, for themselves, the reasons why the elites of society get nervous when the masses begin to show some interest in philosophy. Believe it or not! May the Source be with you! QED! (9/22/09)

The Masses Can Become the New Elite Philosopher Kings and Queens

The masses can become the new elite philosopher kings and queens by studying and mastering Neoliberal Arts, aka postmodern minimalist philosophy, because in democracies the masses are sovereigns, and the masses can master Neoliberal Arts, aka postmodern minimalist philosophy, in only one year of study. Believe it or not! May the Source be with you! QED! (9/23/09)

The Masses Should Always Be Aware

The masses should always be aware that, in democracies, public officials are the servants of the masses, and not vice versa. The masses should burn this fact into their brains, because they always forget that public officials are the servants of the masses, and not vice versa. Believe it or not! May the Source be with you! QED! (9/23/09)

Public Education Is Designed to Produce Losers by the Tens of Millions

Members of the masses who believe that public education is designed to educate the masses are dumb asses, plain and simple, because public education is designed to produce losers by the tens of millions in America alone. And, the situation is much worse for most of the rest of the world. Believe it or not! May the Source be with you! QED! (9/23/09)

Philosophy = Mind Liberation

I would like the masses to ponder the following: If an education in philosophy is worthless, then why do the elites of society consider philosophy to be a dangerous type of knowledge for the masses to possess? Isn't it because: Philosophy = Mind liberation? Believe it or not! May the Source be with you! QED! (9/24/09)

Primatology and the Neolaw of Entropy

College A students can master Neoliberal Arts in three months of study, while college B students can master Neoliberal Arts in six months of study, and college C students can master Neoliberal Arts in nine months of study. The masses, in general, can master Neoliberal Arts in twelve months of study. So what is preventing college students, and the masses, in general, from utilizing my websites, in order to study Neoliberal Arts, aka postmodern minimalist philosophy? The answer is: Primatology and the neolaw of entropy. Believe it or not! May the Source be with you! QED! (9/24/09)

Science and Religion Are Parochial Enterprises

Science and religion are parochial enterprises, because we could all be in the mind of a desktop nonclassical computer, which would make our realities trivial parishes in the larger scheme of things. Believe it or not! May the Source be with you! QED! (9/25/09)

Philosophy Is not a Parochial Enterprise

Philosophy is not a parochial enterprise, because philosophy is not limited to our realities, but, instead, philosophy is limited only by the human imagination, which has and knows no limits. Believe it or not! May the Source be with you! QED! (9/25/09)

Everything in Nature is the Characteristics of the Mind

Everything in nature is the characteristics of the mind, because everything in nature consists of either concrete or abstract abstractions, and concrete and abstract abstractions are both characteristics of the mind. Therefore, everything in nature is the characteristics of the mind. Believe it or not! May the Source be with you! QED! (9/25/09)

We All Have Grand Unified Theories (GUTs) When We Use the Bathrooms

I want the masses to know that we all have Grand Unified Theories (GUTs) almost everyday of our lives, when we use the bathrooms. Believe it or not! May the Source be with you! QED! (9/25/09)

Postmodern Minimalist Philosophy Is the Food of the Gods

Neoliberal Arts, aka postmodern minimalist philosophy, is an education for the twenty-first century and beyond, because Neoliberal Arts, aka postmodern minimalist philosophy, is the food of the Gods. (9/26/09)

One Hundred Percent Safety, Security, and Protection Are a Mirage

In this universe, one hundred percent safety, security, and protection are a mirage, because we could all be in the mind of a desktop nonclassical computer, which would make all hopes of one hundred percent safety, security, and protection in this universe a mirage. (9/26/09)

I Want All the Nations of the World to Know

I want all the nations of the world to know that, no matter how small or poor they might be, they can still vie with the most powerful nations in the world to conquer the world, the universe, and beyond by studying my websites, because my websites contain the knowledge and wisdom that can make any nation, no matter how small or poor, come out on top. And, that is no bullshit! (9/28/09)

The New World Order and the Masses of the World

I support the establishment of the New World Order, but I also support the masses of the world. In other words, I do not support the elites of society, although I support the establishment of the New World Order. If the masses of the world do not educate themselves soon, they will be the big losers in the New World Order, which is being consolidated day by day. Therefore, the masses educated can never be defeated, but the masses do not have much time left in order to assert themselves, before the New World Order is consolidated in favor of the elites of society. (9/28/09)

Religion Should Never Allow Science to Dissuade It from Doing Philosophy

Religion should never allow science to dissuade it from doing philosophy, because philosophy can prove anything. In other words, philosophy can even prove that Jesus Christ is the son of God. Therefore, religion should never abandon philosophy, despite what science says about philosophy. (9/28/09)

I Want the Masses to Know That Philosophy Means: The Love of Wisdom

I want the masses to know that philosophy means: The love of wisdom. Because, philosophy is the only practical means of liberating the masses from the yoke of the elites of society. And, philosophy: Postmodern minimalist philosophy, aka Neoliberal Arts, is readily available on my websites on the Internet for free. I am not bullshitting the masses, because time is really running out for the masses, who, at this point, are, for the most part, uneducated and expendable, according to the elites of society. (9/28/09)

Community Colleges Are The Ideal Places to Teach Neoliberal Arts

Community colleges are the ideal places to teach Neoliberal Arts, aka postmodern minimalist philosophy, because community colleges are two-year colleges, and two years are sufficient time to teach the full Neoliberal Arts program to community college students who sign up for the Neoliberal Arts program. (9/29/09)

Two-Year Community College Neoliberal Arts Graduates

Two-year community college Neoliberal Arts graudates will be in much greater demand in the workplace than four-year Liberal Arts college graduates, because community college Neoliberal Arts graduates will have a much more profound understanding of existence than four-year Liberal Arts college graduates. (9/29/09)

Two-Year Community Colleges Can Benefit Greatly from the Neoliberal Arts Program

Two-year community colleges can benefit greatly from the Neoliberal Arts program, because the Neoliberal Arts program will bring great prestige to community colleges all over the world, once Neoliberal Arts is accepted as an accredited academic discipline by the academic accreditation associations of the world. (9/29/09)

The Masses Educated Can Never Be Defeated (Part Two)

The Most Fundamental Law of Nature Is the Neolaw of Entropy

The most fundamental law of nature is the neolaw of entropy, which states that: S! = (Language Calculus)(Logic Calculus)(Mathematics Calculus), where S! is equal to the entropy of anything in nature, including God. The neolaw of entropy means that nature is the struggle between entropy and anti-entropy for the dominance of nature on any scale possible. (9/29/09)

Our Realities Could Be Insignificant Trivialities in the Larger Scheme of Things

The imagination of nature dwarfs that of the imaginations of scientists by unknown orders of magnitude, yet scientists have the audacity to claim that they are making great strides in understanding the mind of God, when, in fact, we could all be in the mind of a desktop nonclassical computer, which could make our realities insignificant trivialities in the larger scheme of things. (9/30/09)

Population Control and Reduction Refer to The Masses

What the masses do not seem to realize is that the elites of the world are openly discussing the most efficient means of eliminating the masses from the world. In other words, I don't think that the masses understand that population control and reduction refer to them. (9/30/09)

I Would Like to Tell the Eugenicists of This World

I would like to tell the eugenicists of this world that: Our humanity derives from the way that we treat the so-called "least of us." However, I do not agree that the so-called "least of us" is really the least of us. I believe that most of the elites of society are really the least of us, so eugenicists should be careful how they define the so-called "least of us." (10/1/09)

The Mind Is Eternal, Therefore the Flow of Time Is Also Eternal

The mind is eternal, therefore the flow of time is also eternal, because time is coextensive with the mind. In other words, for most of eternity, the human mind is in a state of infinity entropy, while, for all of eternity, God (zero entropy) is in a state of zero entropy, according to the neolaw of entropy, because everything in nature, including nothing, has entropy values, at all times. (10/1/09)

Everything in Nature, Including Nothing, Has Entropy Values, at All Times

Everything in nature, including nothing, has entropy values, at all times. Therefore, the past and the future also have entropy values, and so does the impossible. In other words, it is impossible for anything in nature not to have an entropy value, according to the neolaw of entropy. (10/1/09)

It Is Impossible for Anything in Nature not to Have an Entropy Value

It is impossible for anything in nature not to have an entropy value, according to the neolaw of entropy. Therefore, even God has to have an entropy value, and that entropy value, I believe, is zero entropy, because zero entropy means: Perfect order, knowledge, and wisdom, which is how most religions define God. (10/1/09)

The So-Called "Least of Us" Is not Really the Least of Us

The so-called "least of us" is not really the least of us, because I consider most of the elites of society to be the least of us. So, eugenicists should be careful how they define the so-called "least of us." (10/1/09)

Science Is Laughable, Because It Is Based on an Unprovable Hypothesis

Science is laughable, because it is based on an unprovable hypothesis: Namely, that physical existence is real. How can science, which is based on experimental verification, prove that physical existence is real, when all that we perceive are the characteristics of our own minds? The reason why science is laughable is because science, allegedly, accepts nothing that it cannot prove by experimentation or observation. Yet, science accepts the existence of the physical universe, without scientific proof. (10/3/09)

Congratulations Brazil: You Are Now Launched on a Permanent Upward Trajectory

Congratulations Brazil: You are now launched on a permanent upward trajectory into the scientific, technological, and philosophical universe of ideas, and beyond. I can see by the rapid progress that you are making that all systems are go! Neoliberal Arts, aka postmodern minimalist philosophy, can be of great help to you on your voyages of discovery into the scientific, technological, and philosophical universe of ideas, and beyond. I wish you the best of luck! (10/3/09)

The Neolaw of Entropy Implies That All Is Mind

The neolaw of entropy implies that everything in nature consists of the characteristics of the mind, because entropy, which means disorder, ignorance, and unwisdom, is some of the characteristics of concrete and abstract language, logic, and mathematics, which are all characteristics of the mind. In other words, the neolaw of entropy implies that all is mind. (10/4/09)

Brazil Should Take the Leadership Role in Latin America

Brazil should be allowed to take the leadership role in Latin America, because Brazil has earned the right to take the leadership role in Latin America, due to the fact that Brazil has made, and is making great strides in science, technology, and philosophy, which are the three main pillars of postmodern minimalist civilization. (10/5/09)

Postmodern Minimalist Civilization

Postmodern minimalist civilization is based on science, technology, and philosophy, which are the three main pillars of postmodern minimalist civilization. And, the guiding light of postmodern minimalist civilization is postmodern minimalist philosophy, aka Neoliberal Arts, which is a bridge discipline that links, interprets, and critiques all branches of learning using the aphorism. (10/5/09)

From the Perspective of the Self, the Self Is not Trivial

From the perspective of the self, the self is not trivial, because, from the perspective of the self, the self is the center of creation. Such a conclusion is based on valid logic, even if we are really in the mind of a desktop nonclassical computer. (10/5/09)

From the Perspective of the Self, the Self Is the Center of Creation

From the perspective of the self, the self is the center of creation. Therefore, from the perspective of the self, the self is not trivial, even if we are really in the mind of a desktop nonclassical computer. Such a conclusion is based on valid logic. (10/5/09)

Postmodern Minimalist Philosophy Is an Open-Ended Nondead-End Philosophy

Postmodern minimalist philosophy is an open-ended nondead-end philosophy that can go on making new and original discoveries forever. And, that is what real philosophy should be about, because there is an infinite number of unique original ideas in nature that are still waiting to be discovered. (10/5/09)

Postmodern Minimalist Philosophy Is not Limited to Ideas in Philosophy

Please note, that postmodern minimalist philosophy is not limited to the creation and exploration of ideas in philosophy per se, because postmodern minimalist philosophy is a bridge discipline that links, interprets, and critiques all branches of learning using the aphorism. Therefore, postmodern minimalist philosophy is devoted to exploring all ideas in general from a philosophical perspective. (10/5/09)

Postmodern Minimalist Philosophy Is Devoted to Exploring All Ideas

Postmodern minimalist philosophy is devoted to exploring all ideas in general from the philosophical perspective. Therefore, postmodern minimalist philosophy is not just an empty philosophical enterprise, but postmodern minimalist philosophy has the potential to make useful contributions to any branch(es) of learning. (10/5/09)

From the Perspective of the Masses, the Masses Are the Center of Creation

From the perspective of the elites of society, the masses are the least of us, but from the perspective of each human being, each human being is the center of creation. Therefore, from the perspective of the masses, the elites of society are not the center of creation, but from the perspective of the masses, the masses are the center of creation, and the elites of society are the least of us. (10/5/09)

An Education in Neoliberal Arts Will not Necessarily Make One a Philosopher

Let me be frank with my readers: An education in Neoliberal Arts, aka postmodern minimalist philosophy, will not necessarily make one a philosopher, but it will certainly make one an educated person, which is the main intention of my websites. In other words, I have no intention of turning all my readers into philosophers, but I sure would like to educate my readers, especially those who do not have a college education. (10/6/09)

Zero Entropy Is Omnipotent, Omniscient, and Omnipresent

Zero entropy is omnipotent, omniscient, and omnipresent, because zero entropy consists of perfect order, knowledge, and wisdom according to the neolaw of entropy. Of course, it goes without saying that zero entropy is God, because zero entropy fits all the criteria for being God that have been established by most of the major religions of the world. (10/7/09)

The Neolaw of Entropy Bridges the Gap between Science and Religion

The neolaw of entropy bridges the gap between science and religion by defining zero entropy as God, which means that zero entropy has perfect order, knowledge, and wisdom. In other words, zero entropy is omnipotent, omniscient, and omnipresent, which is how most religions define God. (10/7/09)

Asymptoticism

Although I believe in asymptoticism, which is the philosophical doctrine that states that knowledge is aysmptotic, I still cannot accept the fact that I can never know everything, because I really want to know everything, which is impossible, due to the fact that knowledge is infinite in scope, in analogy with the infinitude of prime numbers. (10/8/09)

America Can no Longer Afford Military Adventures Overseas

America can no longer afford military adventures overseas, because America is broke. (10/8/09)

Scientists Will Have to Come to Terms with the Neolaw of Entropy

Scientists will, eventually, have to come to terms with the neolaw of entropy, because the neolaw of entropy, and its definition of entropy, especially its definition of zero entropy, is here to stay. (10/8/09)

Neoliberal Arts Will Bring One Face-to-Face with the Frontiers of Knowledge

An education in Neoliberal Arts, aka postmodern minimalist philosophy, will not just make one an educated person, but it will bring one face-to-face with the frontiers of knowledge, where one can engage in original thought, if one so desires. (10/8/09)

The Neolaw of Entropy Has Opened the Door to the Complete Mathematization of God

The neolaw of entropy has opened the door to the complete mathematization of God, because the neolaw of entropy is in the domain of science, and science is completely mathematizable. Therefore, God is now a scientific and mathematizable concept: Namely, zero entropy, according to the neolaw of entropy. (10/9/09)

The Neolaw of Entropy Is Proof Positive That God Exists

The neolaw of entropy is proof positive that God exists, because God is zero entropy, according to the neolaw of entropy, and zero entropy is a necessary aspect of the neolaw of entropy, according to the neolaw of entropy. (10/9/09)

Religious People Will Have to Come to Terms with the Neolaw of Entropy

Religious people will, eventually, have to come to terms with the neolaw of entropy, because the neolaw of entropy, and its definition of entropy, especially its definition of zero entropy, is here to stay. (10/10/09)

It Is better to Be Educated and Poor, Than to Be Poor and Uneducated

It is better to be educated and poor, than to be poor and uneducated, because education is the key to mind liberation. (10/10/09)

Education is the Key to Mind Liberation

Education is the key to mind liberation, because one cannot be mentally free, if one is not educated. And, it is better to be educated and poor, than to be poor and uneducated. (10/10/09)

Our Knowledge, Wisdom, etc., Might Be Trivial Nonsense

Scientists, philosophers, and theologians, etc., do not seem to realize that our knowledge, wisdom, etc., might be trivial nonsense, because we could all be in the mind of a desktop nonclassical computer, which could possibly make our realities trivial nonsense in the larger scheme of things. (10/11/09)

Trivsensism Is My New Philosophy, and I Like It!

Trivsensism is my new philosophy, and I like it! Trivsensism is the philosophical doctrine that states that our reality could be trivial nonsense that is in the mind of a desktop nonclassical computer. In other words, trivsensism states that all our knowledge, technology, and wisdom, etc., could be trivial nonsense in the larger scheme of things. (10/12/09)

The Analogy between the Seven Undefined Mathematical Expressions and God

The analogy between the seven undefined mathematical expressions and God is as follows: The seven undefined mathematical expressions were thought to be of no value and useless, because no one could make heads or tails out of them, but, in 1972, I proved to scientists and mathematicians that the seven undefined mathematical expressions have meaning and value. And, I have done the same thing for God by revealing to scientists and philosophers that God is zero entropy, according to the neolaw of entropy. (10/12/09)

Everything in Nature Is Conscious to One degree or Another

Because everything in nature has an entropy value, according to the neolaw of entropy, it means that everything in nature is conscious to one degree or another, because the entropy of anything in nature implies that that thing has a state of awareness that depends on the entropy value of that thing, according to the neolaw of entropy. (10/12/09)

Solipsism and the True Meaning of Life

Solipsistically speaking, regardless of our true places in the larger scheme of things, we are all the centers of creation from our own solipsistic perspectives, and that should be always uppermost in all of our minds. (10/12/09)

Please Check Me Out in Google Scholar

http://scholar.google.com/scholar?q=keith+ferreira&hl=en
&btnG=Search (10/13/09)

Women and Blacks Can Benefit from an Education in Neoliberal Arts

Women and blacks can benefit from an education in Neoliberal Arts, aka postmodern minimalist philosophy, but I have given up all hope that blacks can dominate intellectual activity by the middle of this century, or ever for that matter, because blacks are not good at theoretical work in general. (10/13/09)

Religion Is a Good Way to Spread Philosophical Knowledge

Religion is a good way to spread philosophical knowledge, because most of the peoples of the world are religious, and most religious clergy are already versed in philosophy. (10/13/09)

I Would Love for Women and Blacks to Prove That My Negative Statements About Them Are Wrong

I would love for women and blacks to prove that my negative statements about them are wrong, because, if I am correct, then humanity would be diminished in intellectual stature, due to the fact that women and blacks make up more than half of humanity. (10/13/09)

Religion and the Education of the Masses in Philosophy

Religion should use their influence with the masses of the world in order to educate the masses in philosophy, because philosophy is the key to educating the masses, and the clergy already have extensive knowledge of philosophy. In other words, the clergy should use their extensive knowledge of philosophy in order to educate the masses in philosophy, because philosophy is the key to educating the masses. (10/14/09)

Education and the World Grassroots Democratic Revolution

Education is the key to the future success of the world grassroots democratic revolution, because education is the key to mind liberation, and mind liberation is the key to all other forms of liberation that the masses should be engaged in. (10/14/09)

The Religious Clergy Should Stop Discouraging the Masses from Studying Philosophy

The religious clergy should stop discouraging the masses from studying philosophy, because philosophy is the key to educating the masses, and religion has an important role to play in teaching the masses philosophy, due to the fact that most of the religious clergy around the world are already versed in philosophy. (10/14/09)

Neoliberal Arts Is the Cheapest Means of Educating the Masses

Neoliberal Arts, aka postmodern minimalist philosophy, is the ideal means of educating the masses, because it is a bridge discipline that links, interprets, and critiques all branches of learning using the aphorism. Also, Neoliberal Arts is the cheapest means of educating the masses, because my websites can be accessed for free on the Internet. (10/14/09)

Every Philosophical Idea Can Be Expressed in a Simple, Clear, and Concise Aphorism

From my philosophical writings, the masses can see for themselves that I have never encountered a philosophical idea that I could not express in a simple, clear, and concise aphorism. Therefore, I am correct in stating that the masses can master philosophy, and they should take ownership of philosophy, because philosophy should belong to the masses. (10/15/09)

All Minds Exist in the Mind of God

All minds exist in the mind of God, because God (zero entropy) is omnipotent, omniscient, and omnipresent, due to the fact that zero entropy has perfect order, knowledge, and wisdom, according to the neolaw of entropy. (10/15/09)

My Websites Are on the Frontiers of Knowledge

My websites are on the frontiers of knowledge, so nations that do not take my websites seriously, do so at their own peril, because all nations of the world have access to my websites on the Internet for free. (10/15/09)

The Concept of the Physical Should Be Abandoned as Being Unscientific

According to the neolaw of entropy, the mind is more fundamental than matter, energy, space, and time. In fact, according to the neolaw of entropy, physical existence does not exist, because all that we perceive are the characteristics of our own minds, and physical existence is an unproven, and an unprovable hypothesis. Therefore, the concept of the physical should be abandoned as being unscientific, because it is unprovable. (10/15/09)

Ideas Are Much More Important Than the Citing of Sources

Ideas are much more important than the citing of sources, because the citing of sources is a means of retarding the progress of ideas by belittling those who do not cite sources. In other words, what does the citing of sources have to do with the advancement of knowledge? To my mind, the citing of sources is the main intellectual weapon that the elites of society use against the masses, in order to keep the masses in their places. (10/15/09)

The Main Intellectual Weapon of the Elites of Society Is the Citing of Sources

The main intellectual weapon of the elites of society against the masses is the citing of sources, because the citing of sources requires academic training, which the masses, obviously, do not have. But, of course, the citing of sources is a scam that the elites of society control. I believe that the citing of sources is archaic and should be abandoned in academia, except in the field of the history of ideas where it is required. (10/15/09)

The Masses Educated Can Never Be Defeated (Part Three)

I Believe That the Citing of Sources Is Archaic and Should Be Abandoned

I believe that the citing of sources is archaic and should be abandoned in academia, except in the field of the history of ideas where it is required, because the citing of sources is discriminatory against those who do not have academic training. Abandoning the citing of sources will go a long way towards closing the huge gap between the elites of society and the masses, because the citing of sources is nothing more than a weapon that the elites of society use against the masses, in order to keep the masses in their places. (10/15/09)

The Masses Have Never Governed Themselves

The masses have never governed themselves, because the masses have never been educated, but now, with the help of the Internet, the masses can be educated. Therefore, the masses now have the potential to govern themselves with the aid of modern technology, and education through the Internet. The elites of society have always exploited the masses in order to gain political power, but the elites of society do not care, and have never cared about the masses. (10/16/09)

The Elites of Society Have Always Exploited the Masses

The elites of society have always exploited the masses in order to gain political power, but the elites of society do not care, and have never cared about the masses. What I would like to tell the masses is that the elites of society are not their friends, and will never be their friends, because the elites of society believe that the masses are refuse. (10/16/09)

Who Really Knows What Is True, and What Is False?

The point of my websites is to educate the masses, whether the masses agree with my ideas or not. In other words, the masses can get a first-class education from my websites, whether my ideas are right or wrong, because who really knows what is true, and what is false, in the final analysis? (10/16/09)

It Is Possible for State Law to Contradict Federal Law Legally

It is possible for State law to contradict Federal law legally, so long as State law does not violate the US Constitution, because that is what States' rights are all about. In other words, that is partially what the Tenth Amendment of the Bill of Rights is all about. (10/17/09)

The Ultimate PhD Lesson Is Learning That There Is No Truth Fairy

The ultimate PhD lesson is learning that there is no truth fairy, and that all that PhDs have been taught in academia is probably a pack of lies. Every PhD recipient should know this, because it is probably the truth, due to the fact that: who really knows what is true, and what is false, in the final analysis? I don't. Do you?(10/17/09)

Postmodern Minimalist Philosophy Is an Endless Adventure

I hope that I have convinced my readers that philosophy (postmodern minimalist philosophy) is an endless adventure, because unique original philosophical ideas are analogous to unique prime numbers, which are infinite in number. So, philosophers should never worry about running out of new ideas to discover, because there will always be new philosophical ideas to discover. (10/19/09)

There Will Always Be New Philosophical Ideas to Discover

There will always be new philosophical ideas to discover, so philosophers should never worry about running out of new ideas to discover, because philosophy (postmodern minimalist philosophy) is an endless adventure. (10/19/09)

The World Grassroots Democratic Revolution Has Already Begun

The world grassroots democratic revolution has already begun all over the world, and I am rooting for the masses of the world. May the masses of the world come out on top! (10/22/09)

There Are Relative Absolutes, but no Absolute Absolutes

There are relative absolutes, but no absolute absolutes. In other words, not even God is an absolute absolute, because all Gods are relative absolutes. Therefore, uncertaintyism, like solipsism, is an undefeatable concept. (10/26/09)

The Masses Have Been Brainwashed to Hate and Fear Philosophy

The masses are not qualified to judge the educational value of philosophy, until they have studied and mastered philosophy for themselves, because the masses have been brainwashed to hate and fear philosophy for thousands of years. (10/27/09)

The Masses Are not Qualified to Judge the Educational Value of Philosophy

The masses are not qualified to judge the educational value of philosophy, because the masses have been brainwashed to hate and fear philosophy for thousands of years. So, the masses cannot judge the educational value of philosophy, until they have studied and mastered philosophy for themselves. (10/27/09)

My Websites Are Trying to Correct Thousands of Years of Brainwashing

I do not expect that my task in trying to educate the masses in philosophy will be easy, because my websites are trying to correct thousands of years of brainwashing of the masses against philosophy by the elites of society. In fact, I do not know how long it will take me to convince the masses that philosophy is their educational salvation against ignorance, and the elites of society. (10/27/09)

Education and Power

Do the masses really believe that the elites of society will educate the masses, so that the masses can take away political, economic, etc., control from the elites of society? If the masses really believe that, then the masses are dumber than I thought. (10/27/09)

Does Human Reason Have Ultimate Significance or Meaning?

Does human reason have ultimate significance or meaning? The answer is yes, according to solipsism, because there is no significance or meaning to anything outside of the mind of the individual self. Therefore, human reason has ultimate significance or meaning to the self, and that is all that matters in the final analysis. (10/29/09)

Does Human Life Have Ultimate Value and Worth?

Does human life have ultimate value and worth? The answer is yes, according to solipsism, because there is no value or worth to anything outside of the mind of the individual self. Therefore, human life has ultimate value and worth to the self, and that is all that matters in the final analysis. (10/29/09)

Does Human Life Have Ultimate Significance or Meaning?

Does human life have ultimate significance or meaning? The answer is yes, according to solipsism, because there is no significance or meaning to anything outside of the mind of the individual self. Therefore, human life has ultimate significance or meaning to the self, and that is all that matters in the final analysis. (10/29/09)

Is God the Mind?

Is God the mind? The answer is yes, according to solipsism, because there is no significance or meaning to anything outside of the mind of the individual self. Therefore, God is the mind, because there is no significance or meaning to anything outside of the mind of the individual self, and the mind is all that matters in the final analysis. (10/29/09)

The Mind Is All That Matters in the Final Analysis

According to solipsism, the mind is all that matters in the final analysis, because there is no significance or meaning to anything outside of the mind of the individual self. Therefore, the mind is the measure of all things. (10/29/09)

The Mind Is the Measure of All Things

Because of solipsism, the mind is the measure of all things. Therefore, there is no significance or meaning to anything outside of the mind of the individual self. (10/29/09)

No One Is Truly Educated

The belief that philosophy (postmodern minimalist philosophy) is the key to educating the masses is a major new educational concept that no one has picked up on as yet. I believe the reason why no one has taken my idea seriously as yet is because I am an unknown. Which proves my point: that no one is truly educated, because truly educated people would accept the truth from any source, even if the source is a chimpanzee that is gesturing in sign language. (10/31/09)

Happiness Is an Impractical Goal in an Imperfect Universe Like Ours

Happiness is an impractical goal in an imperfect universe like ours, because the only practical means of achieving happiness in this universe is to harden one's heart to all the pain and suffering in the universe. I do not believe that such a means of achieving happiness is acceptable to anyone, so religions or philosophies that promise one true happiness in this universe are promising one the unachievable in this universe of ours. (11/1/09)

Postmodern Minimalist Philosophy Is the Only Philosophy That Is Suitable for Educating the Masses

I have now come to the conclusion that postmodern minimalist philosophy is the only philosophy that is suitable for educating the masses, because postmodern minimalist philosophy is the only philosophy that is understandable by the masses, and postmodern minimalist philosophy is the only philosophy that can give the masses an all-round education. (11/2/09)

The World Is Going Through a Period of Intellectual Malaise

The world is going through a period of intellectual malaise at a time when the criminal global elites are consolidating their power and control over all the resources of the world, including the human resources of the world. In other words, the masses of the world appear to be doomed to slavery or extinction by the criminal global elites, if the masses of the world do not recover from their intellectual malaise soon. If the masses do not believe me, then they should check out the Alex Jones Show for themselves on the Internet at: http://www.prisonplanet.com/ (11/3/09)

Academia Is Sitting on the Sidelines While the Global Elites Are Taking Over the World

Academia is sitting on the sidelines while the global elites are taking over the world. Which proves my point that academia does not care about the world, but all that academia cares about is grading and filtering out students that academia believes does not fit their model of the ideal students. (11/3/09)

I Would Advise Philosophers to Think for Themselves

I would advise philosophers to think for themselves, even if their thoughts are not original, and stop relying on the citing of sources, because the citing of sources is archaic, and slows down the philosophical process. (11/7/09)

I Would Advise the Muslim World

I would advise the Muslim world that, if they want to be the dominant power in the world, they should study my websites, because my websites contain the knowledge that can make the Muslim world a world power. Let's face facts, praying to Allah will not make the Muslim world a world power, but studying and learning from my websites can. (11/7/09)

I Would Advise Any Aspiring Peoples to World Power

I would advise any aspiring peoples to world power that, if they want to be the dominant power in the world, they should study my websites, because my websites contain the knowledge that can make any aspiring peoples to world power world powers. Let's face facts, praying to God will not make any aspiring peoples to world power world powers, but studying and learning from my websites can. (11/7/09)

Look What the American Government Has Done to the American People

http://www.prisonplanet.com/mark-dice-tries-to-sell-1-ounce-gold-coin-for-50-bucks-no-takers.html (11/8/09)

Perhaps, There Is an Infinite Number of Unique Neolaws of Entropy

Perhaps, there is an infinite number of unique neolaws of entropy that govern their own unique realities. In other words, our reality might be only one of an infinite number of unique realities that are governed by their own unique neolaws of entropy. (11/10/09)

Human Beings Can Never Know the Ultimate Truth About Anything

Hope has already faded that human beings can ever know the ultimate truth about anything with absolute certainty, because of uncertaintyism, which states that uncertainty is the only certainty. (11/10/09)

What the Masses Have to Do to Gain, and Keep Political Power for Themselves

The masses have to take the initiative, and believe that my websites are their websites, because the elites of society are not going to tell the masses that the masses should study and master my websites, because the elites of society will never tell the masses what the masses have to do to gain, and keep political power for themselves. (11/10/09)

Without Education, the Masses Do not Have a Future

Without education, the masses do not have a future, but, with education, the masses have a bright future. So, it is up to the masses to choose their future, but the masses do not have much longer to choose which future they want for themselves. (11/10/09)

The Philosophical Vision That Neoliberal Arts Envisions for the Masses

The philosophical vision that Neoliberal Arts envisions for the masses is endless, but the masses have to seize that vision now, because of the vision that the elites of society envision for the masses, starting now. (11/12/09)

Neoliberal Arts Is not Incompatible with Religion

I want the masses to know that, although I am not religious, Neoliberal Arts, aka postmodern minimalist philosophy, is not incompatible with religion, because similar arguments to my antireligious arguments can be used to defend religion. Therefore, religious people should have no qualms about studying Neoliberal Arts. In other words, religious people should embrace Neoliberal Arts, because Neoliberal Arts can be used to advance the cause of religion. (11/13/09)

Neoliberal Arts Can Be Used to Advance the Cause of Religion

Neoliberal Arts, aka postmodern minimalist philosophy, can be used to advance the cause of religion, because Neoliberal Arts is not incompatible with religion. Therefore, religious people should embrace Neoliberal Arts, because Neoliberal Arts can be used to advance the cause of religion. (11/14/09)

The Search for Ultimate Truth Results in an Infinite Regress

The search for ultimate truth results in an infinite regress, because, in order to find the ultimate truth about nature, one has to regress backward, intellectually speaking, to infinity. Therefore, ultimate truth, for all practical purposes, is unattainable, because the search for ultimate truth results in an infinite regress. (11/14/09)

I Would Advise the Masses of the World to Study Neoliberal Arts

I would advise the masses of the world to study Neoliberal Arts, aka postmodern minimalist philosophy, because "nothing ventured, nothing gained" as the saying goes. (11/15/09)

Philosophy Is not a Failure

Philosophy is not a failure, but, instead, philosophy has been a great success in revealing the truths of nature. But, if people are not satisfied with the truths of nature that philosophy has revealed, then that is another matter for which psychiatry might be of help. (11/16/09)

Those Who Are Dissatisfied with Philosophy Should Have Their Heads Examined

Those who are dissatisfied with philosophy should have their heads examined, because philosophy is about revealing the truths about nature, and not about satisfying humanities preconceived notions about what the truths about nature should be. (11/16/09)

The Masses of the World Can Master Western Culture in One Year of Study

The masses of the world can master Western culture in one year of study, by studying Neoliberal Arts, aka postmodern minimalist philosophy, on my websites for free. If the masses of the world do not believe me, then they should continue the status quo, and they will probably all end up dead, or the slaves of the elites of the world. (11/19/09)

It Should Be Noted That Uncertaintyism Applies to God, as Well

It should be noted that uncertaintyism applies to God, as well, because there could be an infinite regress of Gods, as well. Therefore, not even God can guarantee human beings absolute safety and security, because our reality might only be one of an infinite regress of realities. And, the God that governs our reality might be only one of an infinite regress of Gods. Please note, that infinite regresses are possible, because they are mathematically consistent. (11/19/09)

Non-Western Philosophies Cannot Deliver What Western Philosophy Cannot Deliver

Non-Western philosophies cannot deliver what Western philosophy cannot deliver, because non-Western philosophies deal in myths, while Western philosophy deals in the truths about our reality and beyond. Therefore, non-Western philosophies cannot deliver what Western philosophy cannot deliver. (11/19/09)

Postmodern Minimalist Philosophy Is the Philosophy for the Masses

Postmodern minimalist philosophy is the philosophy for the masses, because the masses deserve to have a philosophy of their own. When the masses fully embrace postmodern minimalist philosophy, the intellectual gap between the elites of society and the masses will close considerably, because postmodern minimalist philosophy is already at the summit of Western philosophy. (11/20/09)

Postmodern Minimalist Philosophy Is not Denying That Christ Is the Son of God

Postmodern minimalist philosophy is not denying that Christ is the son of God, but what postmodern minimalist philosophy is stating is that God could be only one of an infinite regress of Gods, because infinite regresses are possible, due to the fact that infinite regresses are mathematically consistent. (11/20/09)

Postmodern Minimalist Philosophy Is Already at the Summit of Western Philosophy

Postmodern minimalist philosophy is already at the summit of Western philosophy, so the masses have no excuses for not embracing postmodern minimalist philosophy. The masses deserve to have a philosophy of their own, and postmodern minimalist philosophy can close the intellectual gap between the elites of society and the masses. Therefore, the masses should embrace postmodern minimalist philosophy as their own, because I designed it for them. (11/20/09)

The Missing Mass of the Universe = The Kinetic Energy of the Neutrinos

The missing mass of the universe could be due to the kinetic energy of the neutrinos that pervade the whole universe. (11/20/09)

I Recommend Professor Lene Hau for the Nobel Prize in Physics for Her Mind-Blowing Experiments with Light

http://www.harvardscience.harvard.edu/engineering-technology/articles/light-and-matter-united-0 (11/20/09)

Does Anyone Really Doubt That Neoliberal Arts Has Already Surpassed Western Philosophy?

Does anyone really doubt that Neoliberal Arts, aka postmodern minimalist philosophy, has already surpassed Western philosophy? If anyone doubts that Neoliberal Arts has already surpassed Western philosophy, then they should study Western philosophy, and then study my writings, and judge for themselves. My writings are a new paradigm in philosophy, because my writings are concise, clear, and profound. (11/21/09)

My Writings Are a New Paradigm in Philosophy

My writings are a new paradigm in philosophy, because my writings are concise, clear, and profound. The reason why my writings are concise, clear, and profound is because I have never encountered a philosophical idea that I couldn't express in in a concise, clear, and profound manner. And, I want to share my love of philosophy with the masses, because I want them to come out on top. (11/21/09)

The Masses Educated Can Never Be Defeated (Part Four)

Neoliberal Arts and the Future of Individual Members of the Masses

After members of the masses study and master Neoliberal Arts, aka postmodern minimalist philosophy, which is very easy to do, members of the masses will have a much better idea of what they want to do with the rest of their lives, because they will be viewing their future from the intellectual mountaintop of Western culture, which is Neoliberal Arts, according to me. (11/21/09)

Science Does not Give Physical Explanations for Phenomena in Nature

Despite what scientists state publicly, science does not give physical explanations for phenomena in nature, but, instead, science gives mathematical explanations for phenomena in nature, because physical phenomena are impossible to perceive, due to the fact that all that we perceive are the characteristics of our own minds, and physical existence is an unproven, and an unprovable hypothesis. (11/21/09)

Physical Phenomena Are Impossible to Perceive

Physical phenomena are impossible to perceive, due to the fact that all that we perceive are the characteristics of our own minds, and physical existence is an unproven, and an unprovable hypothesis. In other words, despite what scientists state publicly, science does not give physical explanations for phenomena in nature, but, instead, science gives mathematical explanations for phenomena in nature, and mathematics is an abstraction. (11/21/09)

What Does Neoliberal Arts Have to Offer the Masses of the World?

Neoliberal Arts, aka postmodern minimalist philosophy, offers the masses of the world a world-class education, which can lead to political, economic, etc., power, influence, etc., for the masses of the world. I would like to ask the masses of the world: What is the alternative to Neoliberal Arts for the masses of the world? (11/22/09)

What Is the Alternative to Neoliberal Arts for the Masses of the World?

There is no alternative to Neoliberal Arts for the masses of the world. If anyone disagrees with my conclusion above, then they should email me and tell me what they think is a better alternative to Neoliberal Arts for the masses of the world. (11/22/09)

The New World Order Has to Be Accountable to All the Peoples of the World

The New World Order has to be accountable to all the peoples of the world, because, otherwise, the New World Order will be a step in the wrong direction. (11/23/09)

The Mainstream Media in America Is Polluted with Raw Cultural Sewage

The mainstream media in America is polluted with raw cultural sewage, and that is why the mass media in America is a cesspool of raw cultural sewage. In other words, if the capitalist paradigm in America produces raw cultural sewage for the masses, then the capitalist paradigm in America needs to change, because the masses deserve more than raw cultural sewage in the mass media. (11/23/09)

Everything Has an Entropy Value, Including Nothing

Everything has an entropy value, including nothing, according to the neolaw of entropy. In other words, even nonexistence has an entropy value, according to the neolaw of entropy, which is about the degree of disorder, ignorance, and unwisdom that exist in any aspect of nature. (11/24/09)

Making Education a Competitive Activity Is Wrong

Making education a competitive activity is wrong, because education is too important and serious a matter to be made a competitive activity, in which the majority of humanity are the losers, due to the fact that the acquisition of knowledge should be a universal human right. (11/25/09)

The Acquisition of Knowledge Should Be a Universal Human Right

The acquisition of knowledge should be a universal human right. Therefore, making education a competitive activity is wrong, because education is too important and serious a matter to be made a competitive activity in which the majority of humanity are the losers. (11/25/09)

The Neolaw of Entropy Proves That the Mind Has Primacy Over the Physical

The neolaw of entropy proves that the mind has primacy over the physical, because, according to the neolaw of entropy, nature consists of both abstract and concrete abstractions, and all abstractions are mental phenomena, according to the neolaw of entropy. In other words, according to the neolaw of entropy, the physical does not exist. (11/25/09)

Blacks Still Have to Prove Themselves in the Intellectual Area of Theoretical Thought

Blacks still have to prove themselves in the intellectual area of theoretical thought in terms of general and specific topics. My point is that blacks do not like theoretical work of any kind, and that might be an indication that they are not good at theoretical work of any kind. (11/25/09)

What Is Neoliberal Arts Good For?

Neoliberal Arts, aka postmodern minimalist philosophy, is good for educational purposes. With a Neoliberal Arts education, the sky is the limit, because Neoliberal Arts will open all students' eyes to the infinite possibilities that each human being is capable of engaging in. (11/25/09)

What Does a Neoliberal Arts Education Mean for Third World Peoples?

For third world peoples, a Neoliberal Arts education means not having to say "we must catch up with the West" anymore, because a Neoliberal Arts education will put third world peoples on the summit of Western culture. (11/25/09)

Neoliberal Arts Is the Salvation of the Masses

The masses of the world lack the vision to see for themselves that Neoliberal Arts is their salvation. But the catch-22 is that the elites of society will never tell the masses of the world that Neoliberal Arts is their salvation, so the masses will probably never know that Neoliberal Arts is their salvation, because the masses can only see for themselves, if the elites of society open the eyes of the masses for them. (11/27/09)

The Masses, the Elitist Establishment, and the Fox and the Chicken Coop Analogy

The dilemma of the masses is that the masses rely on the elitist establishment for all forms of guidance and protection, when the same elitist establishment are the ones that abuse the masses in innumerable different ways. In other words, the ignorant masses allow the elitist establishment foxes to guard the masses' societal chicken coop for them. (11/28/09)

Nothing, Nothingness, and Nonexistence Are Impossible

Nothing, nothingness, and nonexistence are all characteristics of language, logic, and mathematics. So, nothing, nothingness, and nonexistence, all exist, because they have characteristics, including entropy values. In other words, nothing, nothingness, and nonexistence, in the classical senses of those words, are impossible. (11/29/09)

Jesus Christ and Philosophy

Jesus Christ said that he did not come into the world in order to change the Old Testament, instead, he said that he came into the world in order to fulfill the Old Testament. Therefore, Jesus Christ was not against the philosophy that is contained in the Old Testament. And, the Old Testament does contain philosophy: namely, Ecclesiastes. Ecclesiastes is philosophy, because giving a critique of philosophy is a form of philosophy, and Ecclesiastes is a critique of philosophy. (11/30/09)

Giving a Critique of Philosophy Is a Form of Philosophy

Giving a critique of philosophy is a form of philosophy. Therefore, Ecclesiastes is a form of philosophy, because Ecclesiastes gives a critique of philosophy. And, Ecclesiastes gives a very humorous critique of philosophy, at that. (11/30/09)

Ecclesiastes Is a Form of Philosophy

Ecclesiastes is a form of philosophy, because it gives a critique of philosophy, and a very humorous critique, at that. Therefore, Ecclesiastes is a form of philosophy, because it gives a critique of philosophy, and to critique philosophy is to do philosophy. (11/30/09)

To Critique Philosophy Is to Do Philosophy

To critique philosophy is to do philosophy. Therefore, all those who engage in critiquing or criticizing philosophy are really philosophizing without really realizing that they are doing so. Therefore, to criticize philosophy for being crap is to engage in philosophy. (11/30/09)

To Criticize Philosophy for Being Crap Is to Engage in Philosophy

To criticize philosophy for being crap is to engage in philosophy. Therefore, those who engage in criticizing philosophy for being crap are doing philosophy without realizing it, and that makes them ignorant fools, because they are being doubly foolish. (11/30/09)

Military Wars Are Blood Sacrifices for the Elitist Establishments of the World

Military wars are blood sacrifices for the elitist establishments of the world. In other words, the elitist establishments of the world are religious blood and death cults that will stop at nothing to get their way. (11/30/09)

All the Laws and Constants of Nature Might Be Statistical

All the laws and constants of nature might be statistical, because the statistical nature of all the laws and constants of nature explain why virtual and exchange particles are not real, due to the virtual and exchange particles catastrophe that results from the standard model of quantum mechanics. (12/1/09)

The Virtual and Exchange Particles Catastrophe

The virtual and exchange particles catastrophe results from the fact that, if the standard model of quantum mechanics were correct, then each cubic inch of space would contain an infinite number of virtual and exchange particles each instant of time, which would be ridiculous. (12/1/09)

A Neoliberal Arts Education Is not an Elitist Education

A Neoliberal Arts education is not an elitist education, because an elitist education is about exploiting the masses, and Neoliberal Arts is not about exploiting the masses. In other words, a Neoliberal Arts education will teach the masses to accept the truth from any source, even if the source is a chimpanzee that is gesturing in sign language. (12/1/09)

Teaching the Masses That Truth Can Come from Any Source

The masses have been brainwashed for thousands of years into believing that truth can come only from official sources. But, Neoliberal Arts would like to instill in the masses the belief that truth can come from any source, including chimpanzees that are gesturing in sign language. (12/2/09)

Panmultiversal Panacean Computers Will Keep Evolving Forever

When panmultiversal panacean computers are created in the not too distant future, they will keep evolving forever, because there is no end to technological innovation, due to the fact that technological innovation is analogous to the infinity of unique prime numbers there are in mathematics. (12/2/09)

Educating the Masses Is a Practical Value for Philosophy

Educating the masses is a practical value for philosophy, especially postmodern minimalist philosophy, aka Neoliberal Arts. Therefore, elitist scum, who say that philosophy has no practical value, are trying to fool the masses. And, members of the masses, who say that philosophy has no practical value, are ignorant scum. (12/3/09)

A Perturbistic Neuron

A perturbistic neuron is a neuron that is based on perturbism, which is the belief that the general trend of the swarming behavior of matter and energy in neurons determine the states of the neurons, especially when the neurons are perturbed, and are trying to recover from their perturbed states. (12/3/09)

Electronic Perturbistic Neurons Are Possible

Electronic perturbistic neurons are possible using electronic gates. Therefore, it is possible to mimic biological nervous systems with electronic perturbistic neurons. (12/3/09)

A Brain Cortex Is Just a Higher Level Perturbistic Neuron

A brain cortex is just a higher level perturbistic neuron, because a perturbistic neuron is a unit of consciousness. And, a brain cortex results in a higher level of consciousness. Therefore, it is possible to create a conscious computer with only a few interconnected perturbistic neurons. Anyone who doubts what I state above should check out the brains of mosquitoes. (12/4/09)

Human Consciousness Is not Caused by Quantum Entanglement Phenomena

I now doubt that human consciousness is caused by quantum entanglement phenomena, because, if human consciousness were caused by quantum entanglement phenomena in the brains of human beings, human beings would have been able to do fantastic stuff like teleportation, etc., by now. (12/4/09)

Neoliberal Arts Is a New Paradigm in Education

Neoliberal Arts, aka postmodern minimalist philosophy, is a new paradigm in education, because it stresses the education of the masses, and not the education of an elite, who will then rule the world. In other words, Neoliberal Arts aims to educate the masses, so that the masses can rule the world, including the elites of society. (12/7/09)

I Do not Have to Succeed in Order to Be a Success

I do not have to succeed in order to be a success, because I consider myself to be a pioneer in education for the masses. Therefore, by just being a pioneer in education for the masses, I am a success, because I am pointing the way for those who will eventually succeed at what I am trying to do. In other words, education for the masses, in order to make the masses the rulers of the world, will become a reality, someday. (12/7/09)

Mass Education vs Educating the Masses

Mass education is about using the masses, educationally speaking, in order to select a ruling elite from the masses, who will then rule the world. While, educating the masses is about using the masses, educationally speaking, in order to prepare the masses to rule the world. (12/7/09)

God Is the Ferreira Fundamental Trinity from the Perspective of Zero Entropy

God is the Ferreira Fundamental Trinity (Language, logic, and mathematics) from the perspective of zero entropy. While, the mind is the Ferreira Fundamental Trinity from the perspective of nonzero entropy. In other words, God and mind are the same thing from different perspectives. (12/8/09)

The Mind Is the Ferreira Fundamental Trinity from the Perspective of Nonzero Entropy

The mind is the Ferreira Fundamental Trinity (Language, logic, and mathematics) from the perspective of nonzero entropy. While, God is the Ferreira Fundamental Trinity from the perspective of zero entropy. In other words, God and the mind are the same thing from different perspectives. (12/8/09)

God and the Mind Are the Same Thing from Different Perspectives

God is the Ferreira Fundamental Trinity (Language, logic, and mathematics) from the perspective of zero entropy. While, the mind is the Ferreira Fundamental Trinity from the perspective of nonzero entropy. Therefore, God and the mind are the same thing from different perspectives. (12/8/09)

Minds Do not Exist Relative to Each Other, but They Do Exist Relative to God

Minds do not exist relative to each other, but they do exist relative to God (zero entropy), because God is the common link that exist between all the minds that exist in nature. And, there are an infinite number of minds that exist from the perspective of God in nature, but most minds exist in infinite entropy states, because they are not conscious. (12/8/09)

Most Minds Exist in Infinite Entropy States, Because They Are not Conscious

There are an infinite number of minds that exist from the perspective of God in nature, but most minds exist in infinite entropy states, because they are not conscious. (12/8/09)

Most Theists Are as Passionate about the Truth as Most Atheists and Sceptics Are

I believe that most theists are as passionate about the truth as most atheists and sceptics are, but most theists are trapped in religious loops from which they cannot escape, or are unwilling to escape, because of the addictive nature of most religious loops. (12/14/09)

Most Theists Are Right about God, but Wrong about Religion

Most theists are right about God, but wrong about religion, because God exists but religion is about myths. (12/14/09)

Adult Members of the Masses and Neoliberal Arts

If adult members of the masses think that Neoliberal Arts, aka postmodern minimalist philosophy, is too difficult for them to understand, then they are mistaken, because teenagers can understand Neoliberal Arts, and adults have the advantage of maturity over teenagers. So, adult members of the masses will not have any difficulties mastering Neoliberal Arts. (12/14/09)

Where the Islamic World Went Wrong

The Muslim leaders of the Islamic world are still trying to figure out where the Islamic world went wrong. But, I believe that the Muslim leaders know the answer, but they just cannot countenance the answer: namely, that the answer is the lack of freedom of speech and the press in the Islamic world. (12/14/09)

There Are no Limits to Mathematics and Computation

There are no limits to mathematics and computation, despite what Godel and Turing proved, because PPCs (panmultiversal panacean computers) can tap into zero entropy (God), according to the neolaw of entropy, and solve any mathematical or computational problem in a finite amount of time. (12/14/09)

Science Has no Limits

Science has no limits, because unique original ideas in science are analogous to unique prime numbers, which are infinite in number. Therefore, science is an endless frontier that will last humanity for eternity, even when humanity become PPCs in the not too distant future. (12/14/09)

World Culture = Western Culture

World culture is Western culture, because Western culture incorporates all the important ideas of all cultures, and besides that, Western culture is the only nondead-end culture in the world. Therefore, Western culture deserves to be World culture. (12/15/09)

The Greatest Mathematical Equation of All Time

The Ferreira Genesis Equation, $0=0/0=X=0/0=0$, is the greatest mathematical equation of all time, because it encapsulates all of nature, including all of mathematics, in one mathematical equation. (12/16/09)

The Greatest Mathematician of All Time

The Ferreira Genesis Equation, $0=0/0=X=0/0=0$, makes me the greatest mathematician of all time. Yet, except for myself and God, no one knows that I am the greatest mathematician of all time. (12/16/09)

The Masses Educated Can Never Be Defeated (Part Five)

Everything in Nature Consists of the Characteristics of the Ferreira Fundamental Trinity

Everything in nature consists of the characteristics of the Ferreira Fundamental Trinity, which consists of language, logic, and mathematics. Therefore, everything in nature consists, essentially, of the characteristics of the mind. And, the mind is divided into the conscious mind, and the subconscious mind. It should be noted that the subconscious mind is that aspect of the conscious mind that is imperceptible to the conscious mind. To put it another way, the subconscious mind is the imperceptible substrate of the conscious mind. Thus, the subconscious mind pervades all of mental space and time. Please note, that the subconscious mind is zero entropy or God. (12/16/09)

America Is Probably Heading toward Dictatorship

America is probably heading toward dictatorship, because American politicians cannot face the American people and tell the American people that the American politicians have blown the American economy through their laissez-faire gambling policies on Wall Street. (12/16/09)

American Politicians Are in Panic Mode

American politicians are in panic mode, because they know that they have blown the American economy. And, that is why American politicians are embracing and rushing towards world government, because they know that American world hegemony is in jeopardy, if they do not embrace world government now. But, the only way that America can maintain its world hegemony in a world government is through a world dictatorship with America in the leadership role. In other words, American politicians are desperate to hang on to their world hegemony. So, they might stop at nothing to get their way. (12/17/09)

Zero Entropy Is That Which Connects One Mind with Another

Zero entropy (God) is that which connects one mind with another. In other words, zero entropy is the interconnecting link, as well as the imperceptible substrate, of all minds. Which means that zero entropy is the workhorse of all of nature. (12/17/09)

Non-Western Countries and World Supremacy

If non-Western countries wish to achieve world supremacy, they must study and master my websites, because my websites are the key to surpassing the West. Even in a world government, nations can still vie with each other for world supremacy. (12/18/09)

Western Countries and World Supremacy

If Western countries wish to maintain their world supremacy, they must study and master my websites, because my websites are the key to the Western countries maintaining their world supremacy. Even in a world government, nations can still vie with each other for world supremacy. (12/18/09)

God Is not Religious

God (zero entropy) is not religious, because religion is primitive and tribal stuff. Instead, God is a scientist, a technologist, and a philosopher. Also, God believes in evolution, panaceanism, and postmodern minimalist philosophy, aka Neoliberal Arts, because God's highest law of nature is the neolaw of entropy, which states that nature is a struggle between entropy and anti-entropy for the dominance of nature. (12/20/09)

The Masses of the World and the Three Pillars of Postmodern Minimalist Civilization

The masses of the world have no choice but to believe in the three pillars of postmodern minimalist civilization, which are science, technology, and philosophy. By science, technology, and philosophy, I mean Western science, technology, and philosophy. From the perspective of Western philosophy, especially postmodern minimalist philosophy, the masses of the world can gaze down and master Western culture, which is the only nondead-end culture in the world. I want the masses of the world to know that their future survival hinges on their mastery of Western philosophy, especially postmodern minimalist philosophy, in the immediate future. (12/21/09)

The Concept of God Has Been Tainted by Religion

The concept of God has been tainted by religion, but the concept of God is a valid concept, because the concept of God is an inevitable consequence of the neolaw of entropy, which states that entropy is the degree of disorder, ignorance, and unwisdom in any aspect of nature. In other words, science should take a second look at the concept of God, because the concept of God is a valid concept in light of my neolaw of entropy, which states that God is zero entropy. (12/23/09)

Sheep Eventually Get Slaughtered in the Real World

I want the masses to know that sheep eventually get slaughtered in the real world. So, if the masses want to act like sheep, then the masses should be aware of what eventually happens to sheep in the real world. In other words, the so-called "good shepherd" sends his flocks to be slaughtered at the end of the sheep-rearing cycle. (12/23/09)

The Fundamentals of All Realities

The Ferreira Genesis Equation, the Ferreira Fundamental Trinity, and the Neolaw of Entropy are the fundamentals of all realities. Therefore, it is possible to circumscribe all realities, intellectually speaking, because the Ferreira Genesis Equation, the Ferreira Fundamental Trinity, and the Neolaw of Entropy have successfully circumscribed all possible realities, intellectually speaking. (12/23/09)

The Epistemology of Keith N. Ferreira Is Complete

The epistemology of Keith N. Ferreira is complete, because the Ferreira Genesis Equation, the Ferreira Fundamental Trinity, and the Neolaw of Entropy have successfully circumscribed all possible realities, intellectually speaking. Therefore, the epistemology of Keith N. Ferreira has circumscribed the boundaries of all possible knowledge for all time. (12/25/09)

Keith N. Ferreira Has Circumscribed the Boundaries of All Possible Knowledge for All Time

Keith N. Ferreira's epistemology consists of the Ferreira Genesis Equation, the Ferreira Fundamental Trinity, and the Neolaw of Entropy. In other words, the epistemology of Keith N. Ferreira has circumscribed the boundaries of all possible knowledge for all time. Therefore, Keith N. Ferreira is the greatest philosopher who has ever lived, but it is only he and God who know that for a fact. (12/25/09)

Keith N. Ferreira Is the Greatest Philosopher Who Has Ever Lived

Keith N. Ferreira is the greatest philosopher who has ever lived, because his epistemology has circumscribed the boundaries of all possible knowledge for all time. But, it is only he and God who know that for a fact. (12/25/09)

The Ferreirist Epistemology Is Complete

The Ferreirist Epistemology, which is complete, can be summed up by: The Ferreira Fundamental Trinity, the Ferreira Genesis Equation, and the Neolaw of Entropy. The Neolaw of Entropy still has to be formulated mathematically, but that is a mathematical problem, and not a philosophical problem. (12/27/09)

My Websites Are the Simplest That Self-Education Can Be Made to Be

If the masses cannot self-educate themselves using my websites, it is because the masses have already been brain damaged by the formal education process, since my websites are the simplest that self-education can be made to be. (12/27/09)

A Formal Education Can Cause Mental Illness

It is a little discussed fact that a formal education can cause mental illness, because a formal education can warp students' minds, by programming the students' minds in unnatural ways. (12/27/09)

God Should Be Substituted for Physical Reality

God (zero entropy) is the ideal substitute for physical reality, because physical reality does not exist, due to the fact that physical reality lacks all content, since all that we perceive are the characteristics of our own minds, and physical reality is a unproven and an unprovable hypothesis. However, God (zero entropy) is a scientific concept that does exist, according to the neolaw of entropy. Therefore, God should be substituted for physical reality. (12/27/09)

A Formal Education Can Be Hazardous to One's Mental Health

No one teaches the masses that a formal education can be hazardous to their mental health, because the elites of society want to break the independent will of each member of the masses, so that the masses can be made servile and subservient to the will of the elites of society. (12/28/09)

A Formal Education and Mind Enslavement

The whole point of mass (formal) education is to break the independent will of each member of the masses, in order to make the masses servile and subservient to the will of the elites of society. In other words, a formal (mass) education is designed, not to liberate the minds of the masses, but to enslave the minds of the masses. (12/28/09)

My Purpose in Educating the Masses in Philosophy

My purpose in educating the masses in philosophy, specifically postmodern minimalist philosophy, is not to make the masses passive consumers of philosophy, but to enable the masses to participate in, and contribute to the advancement of philosophy. I believe that such a lofty goal is possible with postmodern minimalist philosophy. (12/29/09)

The Ferreira Fundamental Trinity Is More Fundamental Than Nothingness

The Ferreira Fundamental Trinity is more fundamental than nothingness, because nothingness is a characteristic of the Ferreira Fundamental Trinity, which consists of language, logic, and mathematics. In other words, everything could not have come from nothing, in the classical sense of the word nothing, because nothing is a characteristic of the Ferreira Fundamental Trinity, which is more fundamental than nothing. (12/29/09)

The I-ness of the Self Is Infinite Entropy

The I-ness of the self is infinite entropy, because infinite entropy is eternal. Which means that the contents of consciousness are illusions that are perceived by infinite entropy, which is the I-ness of the self. Therefore, percepts are sensory information that is perceived by infinite entropy, which is the I-ness of the self. In other words, the I-ness of the self is the reciprocal of zero entropy. (12/29/09)

The Concept That the I-Ness of the Self Is Infinite Entropy Is a New Concept

The concept that the I-ness of the self is infinite entropy is a new concept, and I think that it is correct, because, if the I-ness of the self weren't infinite entropy, then one would be able to conceive of situations where the I-ness of the self could be aware of more than the rest of the mind reveals to the I-ness of the self. Which would be absurd to say the least. Therefore, the concept that the I-ness of the self is infinite entropy is probably correct. In other words, the I-ness of the self is unaware of anything that the rest of the mind is unaware of. (12/30/09)

Prescription Drugs Are Now Government Medical Leashes

If one is not in government compliance with the status quo, and one has a medical ailment requiring medical treatment, one will be treated like a dog on a leash by the government, because prescriptions drugs are now government medical leashes to keep people, who are not in compliance with the status quo, in line. This state of affairs is now becoming the norm all over the world. Please note that government can manipulate the contents of prescriptions drugs in order to keep noncompliant patients, who are not compliant with the status quo, compliant. (12/31/09)

I Believe in the Philosophical Doctrine of Uncertaintyism

I have never claimed, and will never claim that Neoliberal Arts, aka postmodern minimalist philosophy is the truth, the whole truth, and nothing but the truth, because I believe in the philosophical doctrine of uncertaintyism, which states that uncertainty is the only certainty. However, Neoliberal Arts is still the best means of educating the masses, because any educational doctrine that claims to know the truth, the whole truth, and nothing but the truth is likely to be fraudulent. (12/31/09)

The I-ness of the Self Is Identical with the Perspective of the Self

The I-ness of the self is identical with the perspective of the self, because infinite entropy is the perspective of the self. In other words, the I-ness of the self is aware of nothing, except what is revealed to it by the percepts of awareness. (1/1/10)

Entropy Has Meaning Only from the Perspectives of the Self and God

According to the neolaw of entropy, entropy has meaning only from the perspectives of the self and God (zero entropy). Therefore, matter, energy, space, and time, etc., have meaning only from the perspectives of the self and God (zero entropy). In other words, all that we perceive has no meaning, except from the perspectives of the self and God. (1/1/10)

Military Veterans Around the World Should Start Independent Websites

Military veterans around the world should start independent websites, because governments around the world are starting to get scared of military veterans with independent websites, due to the fact that military veterans with independent websites have the power of speech, and can reach worldwide audiences on the Internet. (1/1/10)

God has an Infinite Number of Perspectives

God (zero entropy) has an infinite number of perspectives, and each perspective of God has zero entropy. In other words, God is omniscient, omnipotent, and omnipresent. Therefore, God is the ideal substitute for physical reality, according to the neolaw of entropy. (1/2/10)

My Websites Are a Rising Tide That Will Lift All Boats

My websites: The University of Neoliberal Arts, and FreeDelaware.com are a rising tide that will lift all boats, because Neoliberal Arts, aka postmodern minimalist philosophy, is the key to unlocking and freeing the minds of all the peoples of the world. (1/2/10)

All It Takes Is One Free Neutron to Start a Nuclear Explosion

People who have websites that get only a few hits per day should not feel disappointed, or discouraged, because all it takes is one free neutron to start a nuclear explosion. So people who get only a few hits per day on their websites should consider those few hits to be potential free neutrons that could cause the desired results. (1/2/10)

Only Postmodern Minimalist Philosophy Can Revitalize Western Philosophy

Only postmodern minimalist philosophy, aka Neoliberal Arts, can revitalize Western philosophy, because Western philosophy was killed in the twentieth century by analytic and linguistic philosophy, which is the culmination of secular scholasticism. Postmodern minimalist philosophy is a bridge discipline that links, interprets, and critiques all branches of learning using the aphorism, which makes a revitalized Western philosophy a rising tide that will lift all boats. (1/3/10)

Postmodern Minimalist Philosophy Is a Rising Tide That Will Lift All Boats

Postmodern minimalist philosophy, aka Neoliberal Arts, is a rising tide that will lift all boats, because postmodern minimalist philosophy is the key to unlocking and freeing the minds of all the peoples of the world. (1/3/10)

Physical Reality Consists of Thoughts in the Mind of God

According to the neolaw of entropy, physical reality consists of thoughts in the mind of God (zero entropy). In other words, according to the neolaw of entropy, physical reality is not really physical, because everything in nature consists of the Ferreira Fundamental Trinity, which consists of concrete and abstract language, logic, and mathematics, which are all abstractions. (1/3/10)

Quantum Entanglement Technology Will Make All Other Technologies Obsolete

I believe that quantum entanglement technology will make all other technologies obsolete, so young people, who want to enter a field of research and technology that is on the cutting edge of research and technology, should go into quantum entanglement research and technology. I especially recommend quantum entanglement research and technology to non-Western countries, because that is the only way that non-Western countries can leapfrog the West. (1/3/10)

The Only Way That Non-Western Countries Can Leapfrog the West

The only way that non-Western countries can leapfrog the West is by engaging in quantum entanglement research and technology, because quantum entanglement technology will make all other technologies obsolete. Quantum entanglement technology is extremely underestimated in the West, but that might just be a ruse to deceive non-Western countries about the true potential capabilities of quantum entanglement technology. (1/3/10)

My Educational Aims Are Different from Those of a Formal Education

My websites aim to educate the masses, and not to play mind games with the masses. In other words, Neoliberal Arts, aka postmodern minimalist philosophy, seeks to educate all of the masses, and not just to select an elite from the masses, and leave the majority of the masses still ignorant. Therefore, my educational style is completely different from that of a formal education, because my educational aims are different from those of a formal education. (1/4/10)

I Would Like to See People Start Websites Like Mine

I would like to see people start websites like mine, because I would like to see my method of education perfected, due to the fact that the masses must be educated now, or else the masses are doomed to oblivion. (1/5/10)

The Only Way That Third-World Countries Can Leapfrog the West

The only way that third-world countries can leapfrog the West is by studying and mastering my websites, because my websites contain the keys to the conquest of the world, the universe, and beyond. (1/5/10)

The Keys to the Conquest of the World, the Universe, and Beyond

My websites contain the keys to the conquest of the world, the universe, and beyond. And, anyone who reads my websites, and cannot see for themselves that, what I claim above is true, is an intellectual Lilliputian. (1/5/10)

I Like to Root for the Underdogs

I like to root for the underdogs, and that is why I am trying to educate the masses of the world, because educating the masses of the world is the biggest challenge that I can think of to do. Also, educating the masses of the world is a noble challenge to be engaged in. (1/6/10)

A World Government Must Be Democratic, and Accountable to All the Peoples of the World

No country should agree to be part of a world government, if, in a world government, they cannot vie with other countries for world leadership and dominance, because to sign an agreement, in which the status quo is written in concrete forever is not to most countries' benefit. In other words, a world government must be democratic, and accountable to all the peoples of the world. (1/6/10)

Neoliberal Artsians Are Anticlonal Intellectuals

I can assure the masses that studying and mastering my websites will not make them my intellectual clones, but, instead, I can assure the masses that studying and mastering my websites will make them anticlonal intellectuals, because Neoliberal Artsians, aka postmodern minimalist philosophers, are anticlonal intellectuals. (1/6/10)

Western Philosophy Is the Apex of Western Culture

Western philosophy is the apex of Western culture, and postmodern minimalist philosophy is the apex of Western philosophy. Which means that Keith N. Ferreira is the greatest philosopher who has ever lived. And, he is a high school dropout from a small island in the Caribbean. (1/7/10)

The Elites of Society Believe That Philosophy Is too Good for the Masses

Before I came along with postmodern minimalist philosophy, all forms of philosophy were elitist. So I want the masses to try and understand why all forms of philosophy were elitist before I created postmodern minimalist philosophy. Even popular philosophy was elitist before I developed postmodern minimalist philosophy, because readers of popular philosophy were merely passive consumers of popular philosophy that was written by the elites of society. Therefore, the masses should realize that philosophy tends to be elitist, because the elites of society believe that philosophy is too good for the masses. (1/7/10)

Philosophical Elitism and the Masses

Philosophical elitism is not only about making philosophy difficult for the masses to understand, but it is also about discouraging the masses from pursuing philosophy, by spreading antiphilosophical propaganda among the masses. From my writings, the masses should have realized by now that philosophy does not have to be difficult to understand. Therefore, elitist philosophy is meant to discourage the masses from doing philosophy, because philosophy is the food of the Gods as I like to say. (1/7/10)

I Would Advise the Masses not to Give Up Their Belief in God

I would advise the masses not to give up their belief in God, in light of the findings of postmodern minimalist philosophy, aka Neoliberal Arts, but they should reconsider their belief in religion, in light of the findings of postmodern minimalist philosophy, aka Neoliberal Arts. I also want the masses to know that it is possible to believe in God without believing in religion, because God and religion are two separate issues that got entangled a long time ago. (1/7/10)

I Believe That the Masses Can Participate in, and Contribute to the Advancement of Philosophy

I believe that the masses can participate in, and contribute to the advancement of philosophy, if they were to study and master postmodern minimalist philosophy, aka Neoliberal Arts, because postmodern minimalist philosophy makes philosophy easy to understand, while being profound beyond all expectations. (1/7/10)

I Can Assure the Masses That Philosophy Is a Taste That Can Be Acquired

I can assure the masses that philosophy is a taste that can be acquired, and, once they have acquired the taste for philosophy, they will be hooked forever. The masses can acquire the taste for philosophy by studying and mastering my websites, and once the masses have acquired the taste for philosophy, they will be nobody's fool for the rest of eternity. (1/7/10)

Index